How Disk Drives Work

HOW DISK DRIVES WORK

Robert Stetson

How Disk Drives Work

HOW DISK DRIVES WORK

Copyright © 2013 Robert Stetson

All Rights Reserved

Introduction

My objective here is to give you a feeling of understanding, not to make you an expert in the technology.

If you think there should be a lot more pages here, then I will agree that there could have been.

Once you strip away all the mumbo jumbo this is how many pages remain. I didn't fill it with a lot of fluff.

So, here it is in plain English.

How Disk Drives Work

TABLE OF CONTENTS

CHAPTER 1 MAGNETIC DISK DRIVES 1

CHAPTER 2 THE HARDWARE 2

    MAGNETIC DISK DRIVES 2

    FLOPPY DISK DRIVE 6

    RIDGED DISK DRIVE 11

CHAPTER 3 THE SOFTWARE 22

    (DOS) DISK OPERATING SYSTEM 23

    COMMAND LINE 24

CHAPTER 4 CONTROLING A DISK DRIVE 26

CHAPTER 5 THEY ONLY SEEM MAGICAL 35

CHAPTER 1 MAGNETIC DISK DRIVES

The first thing you notice with regard to disk drives is the spelling of the word disc. Having been an Engineer in the disk drive industry since 1980 and served on ANSI (American National Standards Association), ECMA (European Computer Manufacturer's Association) and as a Senior Member of the IEEE (Institute of Electrical and Electronics Engineers), I can tell you that we standardized the name disk to be spelled with a "K".

There are two basic kinds of magnetic disk drives on the market. Of the two types of disk drives, I will explain how they work in simple English.

The first type of disk drive is the Flexible Disk Drive often referred to by the general public as the "Floppy Disk Drive".

The second type of disk drive is the Ridged Disk Drive, often referred to as the Hard Disk Drive.

CHAPTER 2 THE HARDWARE

MAGNETIC DISK DRIVES

The physics behind the reading and writing of the Flexible Disk Drive is essentially the same as the Ridged Disk Drive.

Remember your elementary school science lesson when you slipped a coil around a nail and connected it to a small battery?

The nail could be used to pick up a paper clip.

If the paper clip fell off, it was a temporary magnet.

If the paper clip stayed attached, you made the nail into a permanent magnet.

The coil created the magnet, and the type of metal in the nail determined the type of magnet.

How Disk Drives Work

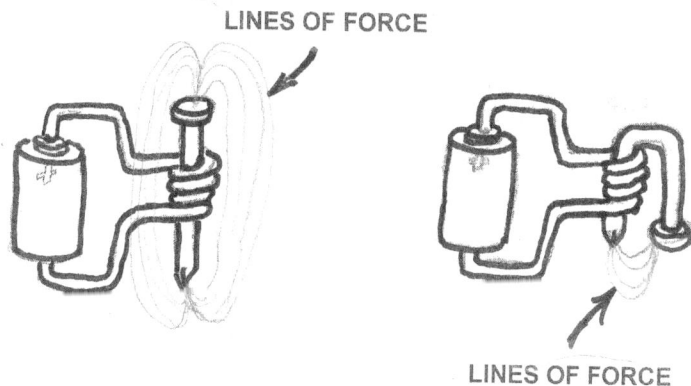

When you create the magnetic force around the nail, it is a large, less dense weak field.

When you bend the nail, you create a smaller gap between the poles and create a smaller, denser focused field.

The read write heads in a disk drive have more of a horseshoe shaped metal core with a much smaller, more focused gap.

Disk drives use a combination of permanent and temporary magnets to control the data content and placement.

The process is simple. Let me show you how they do it.

How Disk Drives Work

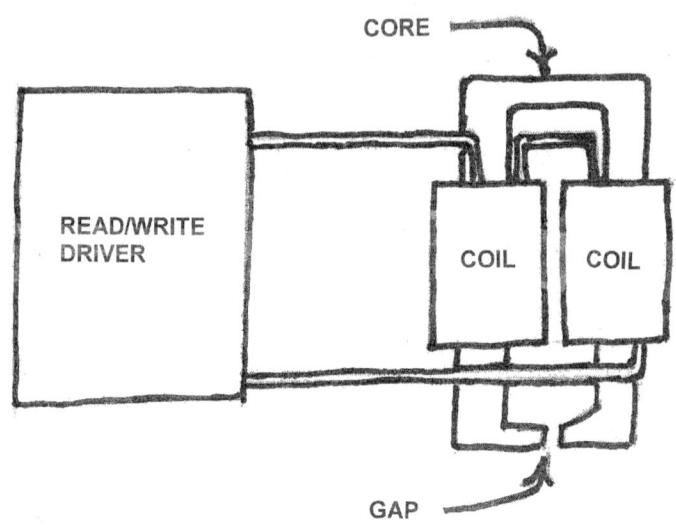

Just as with our example using the nail, we can make a read/write head with a metal core. The disk surface passes underneath the "GAP" and the reversing polarity from the "READ/WRITE DRIVER" will make a reversing magnetic field under the "GAP".

That's only half of the story of how the data is saved. The disk surface tells the other half of the story about how the data signal is stored.

The disk itself is a surface of magnetic iron particles floating in suspension within an emulsion. The emulsion is spread evenly and thinly over a substrate (nonmagnetic surface) and then hardened in the manufacturing process.

The particles can be erased, magnetized in one polar direction or the other and erased again.

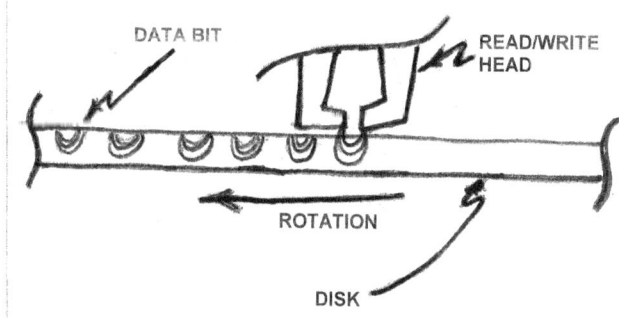

The remnant (remaining) magnetic field will stay on the disk surface until it is erased.

A read/write head passing over the magnetic field will pick up the signal just as it was written.

The iron particles are shaped like rice about three to four times longer than they are wide. They are magnetically aligned on the surface prior to hardening the coating so the disk will be more easily recorded.

FLOPPY DISK DRIVE

Flexible disk drives are no longer popular. They died when the Flash Drive came along.

The head and disk work the same way as a ridged disk drive except the disk is flexible.

These drives have a lower capacity and spin slower than the hard disk.

The heads on a flexible disk are in direct contact with the disk surface.

Positioning the gap on the spinning disk is done by using a stepper motor and a spiral worm-cam to position a ball in the head carriage assembly.

This mechanism is shown in the illustration below.

Stepper motors are high precision devices that have a partial rotation with every pulse. It takes a few steps to rotate one revolution.

The precision cut worm-cam moves the head a small amount for each step of the motor.

The head assembly is shown as a cutaway so you can see the ball guide resting in the spiral cam. The ball-guide is held in the spiral-cam under spring tension from the spring shown on the left.

How Disk Drives Work

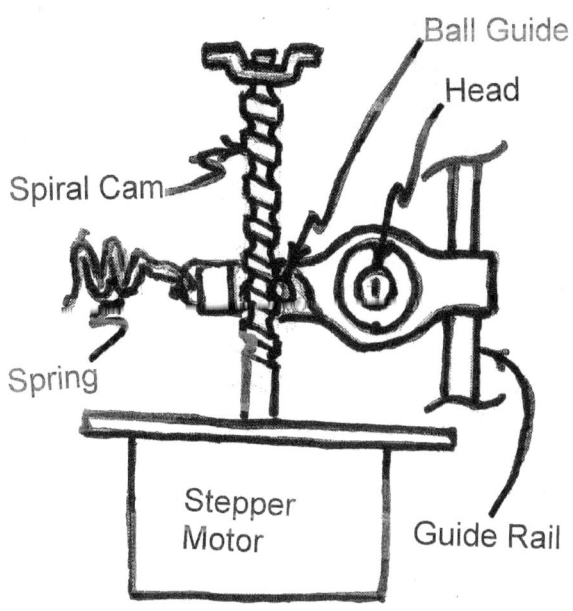

The disk itself is 3.5 inches square with a slide to cover and protect the media surface from dust and dirt.

We figured people would be putting them in their pockets. The pocket is full of lint and crumbs, so we put a spring loaded disk cover on the head opening.

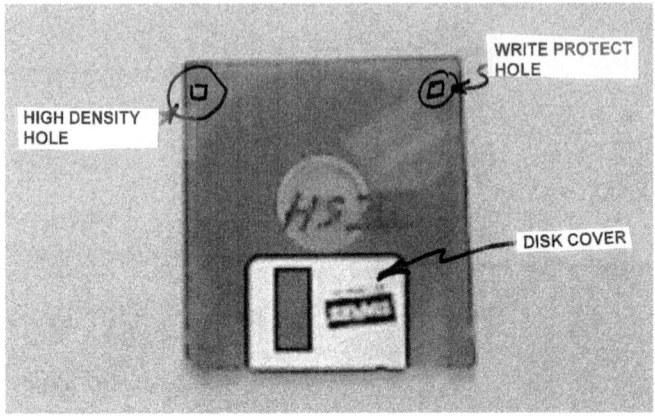

Notice that there are two holes in the top corners of the disk. There are two different capacity disks available. One is low density 1.4 MB and the other is high density 2 MB. The 2 MB disk has a permanent "HIGH DENSITY HOLE" in the corner.

The other corner of the disk has a "WRITE PROTECT HOLE" which has a slide to close it, or pen it. When the hole is closed, the disk is write enabled. When the hole is open, the disk is write protected.

High density (2 MB drives) has a pin to select the high density mode. The pin sticks up through the high density hole. If there is no hole, the drive will operate in low density (1.4 MB) mode.

The low density and high density disks are coated with a different formula for writing, so they are not the same and can't be interchanged by cutting open or covering a high density hole.

How Disk Drives Work

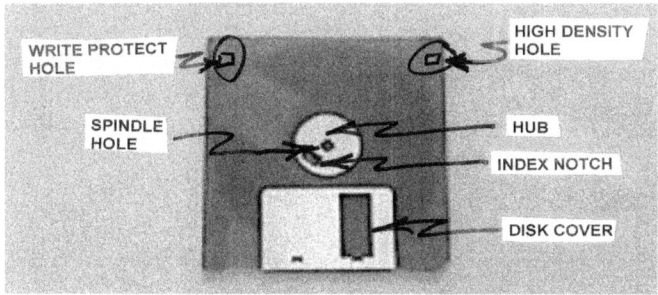

When the disk is inserted I the drive, a lever catches the disk cover and slides it so that the opening in the disk cover aligns with a hole in the plastic jacket.

This exposes the disk surface and the read/write head is brought in and clamps on the disk.

The spindle hole has a pin inserted in it from the motor hub in the drive and the disk is aligned.

A pawl catches the index notch and spins the disk at the proper spin speed.

It's the index notch that establishes the location of the first sector on each track.

Each time the Index Notch passes the location of , the track starting point, an infrared beam is broken and the controller receives a pulse. This pulse is the beginning of the track.

How Disk Drives Work

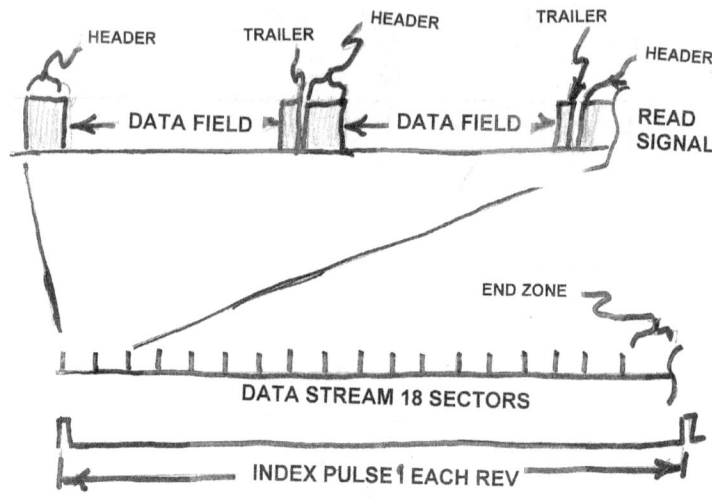

Each track has 18 sectors, so the disk controller starts writing the format when it receives the Index Pulse.

In the case of a read operation, the controller starts reading the track when it receives the Index Pulse and uses the headers to locate each of the 18 sectors.

In a separate operation, the controller begins to read in the pre-formatted headers when it receives the Index Pulse and writes the track within the data window as specified in the sector formatting specification.

RIDGED DISK DRIVE

In terms of functionality, capacity, control systems and general appearance, the ridged disk drive is very different from the flexible disk drive.

On the other hand, data is data and the data fields are the same in both instances.

Both systems have headers and trailers and both systems are more similar than they are different.

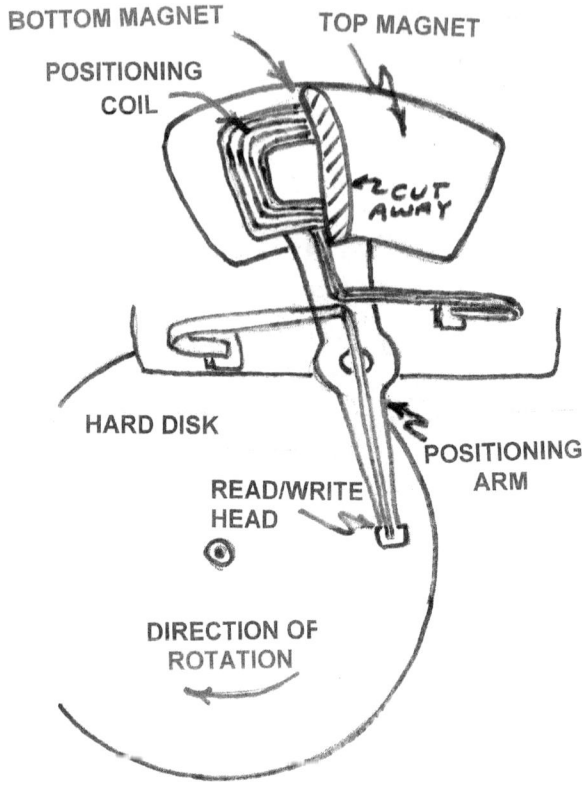

The actual head positioning system is very different in that it is more complex.

Hard disks have a disk surface that is dedicated to servo control.

We can explain the servo loop that keeps the head on the intended track, but just know that the system is dynamic in the way it functions.

As for the read/write and Index pulses, they are the same.

The drive itself is easy to understand if you ignore some of the outwardly unimportant complexities of the unit. It is a plug and play device, after all.

For those of you who want to know more, I have included the following simplified explanation of how the servo system actually works.

The mechanics are fairly simple with only one moving part on each side of each platter.

One side of the first platter is a servo surface that is recorded in a very special way.

I will show you how these servo signals are written and how they provide information to the servo loop to keep the heads in the center of the track

It's important to remember that there is a head and platter stack above the servo platter that align with the head on each track, so the servo motion keeps all of the heads aligned and in the center of their respective tracks.

The servo surface has no data, but its sole purpose is to align the heads above it.

The drawing below shows the permanent magnets which are made of alnico.

If you were to take a hard disk apart and remove this pair of magnets, you might be amazed at how strong they are.

The remarkable strength of these magnets is what allows the heads to position so swiftly.

In the diagram below, the linear motor coil can be magnetized using a current through input lines "A" and "B".

Since like poles attract and unlike poles repel, the head can be moved I one direction or in the other direction by changing the polarity of the "correction signal".

The signal from the servo controller to the head positioning linear motor is just that, a correction signal that is added or subtracted from the linear actuator positioning signal to keep the read/write heads on track.

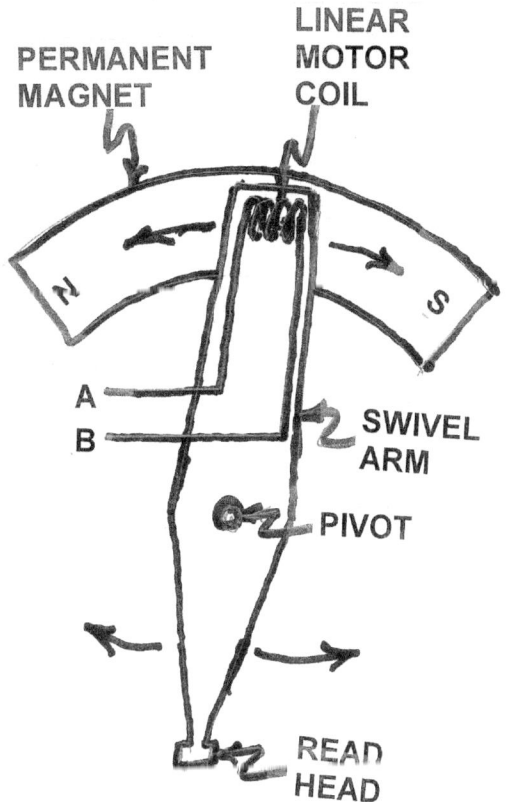

The head positioning drivers output a strong current out of the motor driver to both points "A" and "B" to move the heads to the track location, then the servo loop takes over.

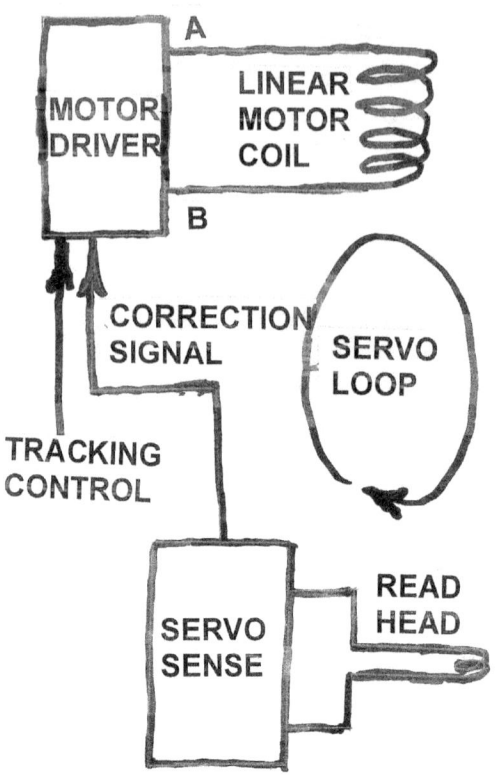

The left hand side of the servo loop is electronic, taking the servo signal from the read head and sensing the head's position relative to the center of the track.

The right hand side of the servo loop is electromechanical, taking the servo driver signal from the motor driver and moving the head's to the correct position relative to the center of the track.

Back at the read head, the track positioning signal has located the track using the track counter ad information located in the data from the track headers, the servo loop takes over.

The servo tracks are written by a servo writer at the factory where the disk drive was manufactured.

These tracks are only written once and never overwritten by the drive. If the servo tracks are damaged, the drive will never work again.

The servo writer will write a burst 50% off-track above and below the track center.

The track begins with an "AGC" burst written on the track center.

When the Index Pulse is received, the servo track head inputs the Automatic Gain Control signal and sets the level of amplification for the servo signal.

If the servo signal is too weak, the offset "OD" and "ID" bursts will be ineffective because they will be missing when reading from the track center and not added properly in the servo sensor.

If the servo signal is too strong, the offset "OD" and "ID" bursts will be ineffective because they will overlap one another in the servo sensor.

You can see the "OD" and "ID" bursts written 50% off track below.

The "T", or "On Track" burst aids in reestablishing the proper amplitude and separate the offtrack signals from one another.

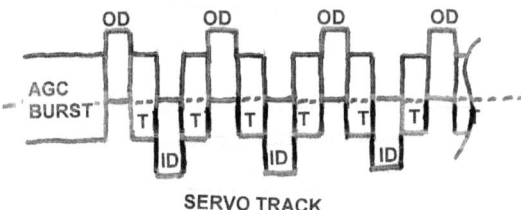
SERVO TRACK

There is a servo track written for every track on the disk. They contain no data and are only intended to keep the read head in the middle of the track.

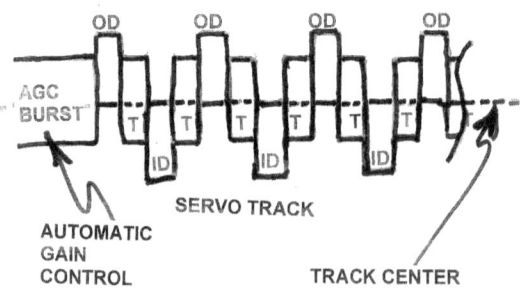
SERVO TRACK
AUTOMATIC GAIN CONTROL
TRACK CENTER

The illustration below shows that the offset "OD" and "ID" bursts are of equal amplitude when the head is in the middle of the servo track.

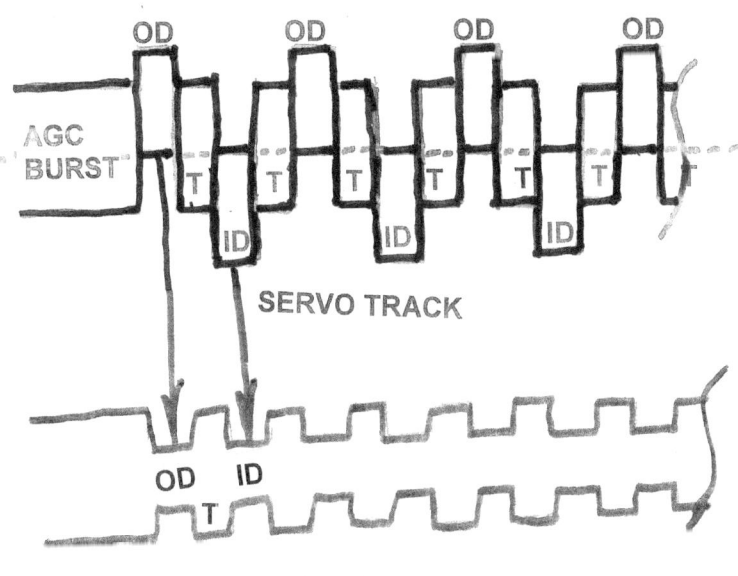

The illustration below shows that when the read head is moved (see the arrow to the left of the servo track) toward the "OD", or Outside Diameter of the disk, the position sensor will see a stronger "OD" signal in the servo sensor. This will create a correction signal out of the servo sensor to the servo driver that will move the heads toward the "ID", or Inside Diameter of the disk.

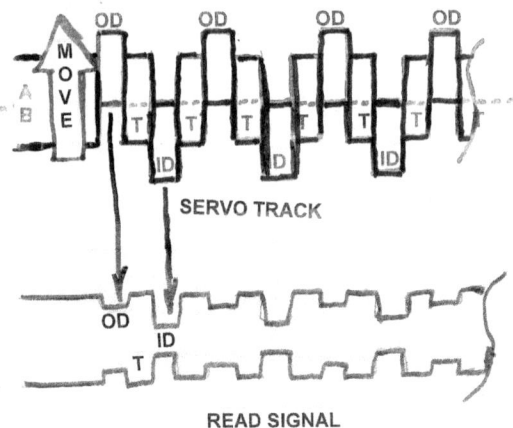

SERVO TRACK

READ SIGNAL

The illustration below shows that when the read head is moved (see the arrow to the left of the servo track) toward the "ID", or Inside Diameter of the disk, the position sensor will see a stronger "ID" signal in the servo sensor. This will create a correction signal out of the servo sensor to the servo driver that will move the heads toward the "OD", or Outside Diameter of the disk.

How Disk Drives Work

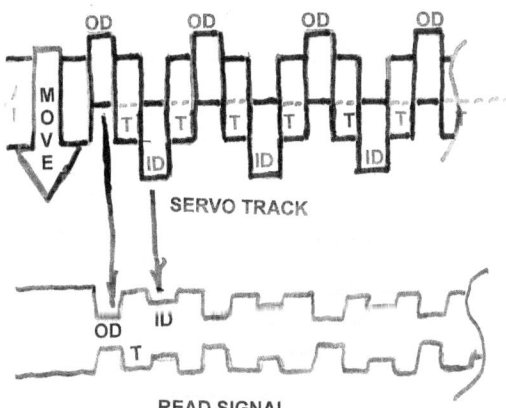

CHAPTER 3 THE SOFTWARE

Just as the flexible disk needs to be formatted before it can be used, so does the ridged disk drive.

The format doesn't really differ very much from the flexible disk drive except that when the drive is initially formatted (initialized) the drive uses the servo to track and position the formatted blocks across all the "platters".

Every disk that's stacked up on the drive is called a platter and is formatted by a different read/write head.

The combination of disks, heads and tracks along with sector numbers (blocks) are just a way of extending the number of tracks available.

If this is all sort of complicated, don't worry about it. The disk drive is just like a huge flexible drive, except it's not flexible and has many disks inside.

(DOS) DISK OPERATING SYSTEM

The disk operating system is not just a software program that runs in the background and is invisible to the user unless you tap into it from the "command line". The Disk Operating System does most of the work. Microsoft has renamed the DOS to the Command Prompt and buried it in the Accessories Window.

The object is to more closely integrate the Command Line Language into the Microsoft Windows environment.

If you hear anyone make reference to DOS, they are probably referring to the pre-Windows-95 version of Microsoft's operating system. That would be DOS 6.22 and Windows 3.11.

COMMAND LINE

The Windows Operating System converts mouse clicks into command line instructions behind the scenes and invisible to the user.

These invisible command line instructions are converted through the disk drive directory information to the various heads, tracks and sectors.

The head selects and servo mechanism positions the read/write head using a "track and sector list" thus identifying the exact location of the file block by block.

They want to discourage the computer user from using the command prompt and rely more on Windows. Many of the old DOS programs no longer works in the computer when running later versions of Windows.

Microsoft claims that the new computer operating systems are backward compatible. When your old programs no longer run after you do an upgrade, Microsoft responds with, "The system is backward compatible. Why would you want to run that old program anyway?"

Thus, Microsoft's question becomes their official answer to your question.

How Disk Drives Work

While the disk is controlled from the windows screen and all you do is click on the various windows to select various disk drives and directories, the disk operating system is the system that knows what to do.

Everything you do on your computer is dealing with files. Even when you are online and looking at the site windows, they are conveyed in the form of HTML files and mapped into the video.

CHAPTER 4 CONTROLING A DISK DRIVE

Disk drive control occurs at the interface where the signal cable plugs into the drive.

There is more than one way to control a disk drive and some are more complicated than others, but the result is the same.

FLEXIBLE DISK DRIVE

Flexible disk drives use a 34 pin ribbon cable to communicate with the drive. The cable carries TTL level signals to and from the drive to operate everything from the side select to the write enable and more.

Although the disk drive has the write enable set at the drive interface, the drive will only write if the disk is write enabled.

All of the functions performed by the drive are controlled by signal lines to and from the drive.

The disk drive controller must perform all of the format read and write functions as well as data transfer and timing.

ST-506 DISK DRIVE

Is the original interface used with the ridged disk drive. Developed by Shugart Technologies, now named Segate Technologies uses a combination of two ribbon cables, a 34 pin ribbon cable and a 20 pin ribbon cable.

Like the flexible disk drive, the disk drive controller did everything and the hard disk is a slave device with no intelligence in the disk drive.

IDE DISK DRIVE

IDE, or Integrated Drive Electronics uses a 40 pin ribbon cable to communicate with the disk drive. The design has been around for a very long time.

The IDE utilizes the ATA, or Advanced Technology Attachment and is relatively unintelligent in its functionality, much like the ST-506.

The largest advantage of the IDE design is the increased data transfer rate along with the more compact design offered by the integrated technology.

The IDE interface embraces a number of different kinds of storage devices from hard disk drives, tape drives to CD and DVD drives and more.

SCSI DISK DRIVE

Another standard interface is the SCSI interface that uses a 50 or 25 pin ribbon cable depending on the type of device.

Like the IDE, the largest advantage of the SCSI design is the increased data transfer rate.

The integrated technology of the SCSI hard disk drive includes a BIOS chip that supports features, such as format capability and on-board diagnostics.

Also, like the IDE interface, SCSI embraces a number of different kinds of storage devices from hard disk drives, tape drives to CD and DVD drives and more.

Another advantage of running SCSI Drives is their ability to support up to 16 devices on a single controller cable.

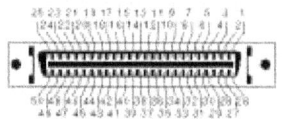

The 50 pin connector

SATA DISK DRIVES

The most popular disk drive interface by far is the 7 pin connector configuration offered by the SATA, or Serial Advanced Technology Attachment **disk drive.**

The Serial Advanced Technology Attachment replaces the parallel ATA used with IDE.

There are currently three levels of SATA with SATA II and SATA III offering better performance.

This is all starting to sound like goble-de-goop if you're just interested in understanding generally how you drive works. Thought I'd throw it in for the folks who wanted a little extra information to follow up on.

The pin-outs for the common SATA 7 pi interface fores like this;

SATA MALE CONNECTOR

Pin 1 Ground

Pin 2 Transmit Data A+

Pin 3 Transmit Data A-

Pin 4 Ground

Pin 5 Receive Data B-

Pin 6 Receive Data B+

Pin 7 Ground

USB DISK DRIVES

External disk drives most commonly use the USB, or Universal Serial Bus 4 pin connector as the interface to the computer.

Inside the external hard drive there is always an adaptor to either an IDE or SATA hard disk drive. This adaptor enables the user to easily connect their hard disk drive to the computer using a common port on the front of the computer.

The following diagram shows the pin-outs for the common USB connector;

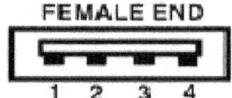

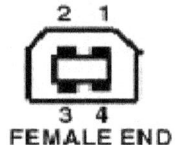

Pin 1 +5 Volts

Pin 2 – Data

Pin 3 + Data

Pin 4 Ground

CHAPTER 5 THEY ONLY SEEM MAGICAL

There is no magic in the way disk drives work. Like any other thing we sometimes take for granted, they are inherently simple once you see how they work.

As you get deeper into the technology, there are highly complex issues that arise and require a great deal of study.

Things like total indicated runout, peak shift, dropouts, remanence and other deeply technical factors enter into it, but the bottom line is still the same. The fundamental operating characteristics of the disk drive are simple.

~~ THE END ~~

www.ingramcontent.com/pod-product-compliance
Lightning Source LLC
Chambersburg PA
CBHW071551170526
45166CB00004B/1634